Psalms of Deliverance

By DORINA HORVATH

DEDICATION

This Book is dedicated to my Lord and Savior Jesus Christ, who is the Author and Finisher of my faith, and my everything. This book was birthed in the darkest season of my life.

FOREWORD

The author recommends first read Psalm 96, for in is the heart of these psalms, and then proceed in chronological order from Psalm 1. This book is written in an old style language so the grammar is intentional. It is a mixture of Old Testament and New Testament scriptures woven together with the deepest cry of the author's heart. When the term Messiah is mentioned, it is a reference to Jesus.

DISCLAIMER

These devotional psalms are not meant to be a dogmatic or theological writing. It is not intended to compete or to be confused with the Book of Psalms from the Old Testament writings. These writings are not meant to be a doctrine but rather transparent reflections of the author's deepest cries interwoven with scriptures.

TABLE OF CONTENTS

Psalm of Deliverance 1

Many a times I was in trouble and sufferings. My soul was near to slip to death. What is not for You I would be in Sheol, but you oh God remain faithful and steadfast. Your mercies are new every morning because that is who You are. Not because of me but because of Your name's sake deliver me and be with me in trouble. I go about mourning day and night. Tears have flooded my eyes. My groanings are silenced by mine enemies. I listen to hear what the Lord will answer me. Will you be angry forever? Will you cast me off into the hand of the enemy? Will you forget your covenant of old? I look every morning if this be the moment that Your word will deliver me. Your word does not return void. Perhaps it is Your word that is trying me in this place. Though I have been snared by mine enemies, and sorrows flooded my soul, yet I will still praise Him. Though you will not deliver, yet I will still praise You. In righteousness You slay and in righteousness You heal. Who can ask You why You do this thing? Our faces are filled with shame for the Lord has punished our iniquities. I remain steadfast in this one thing; it is because of the Lord's mercies that we are not consumed. I will wait to see what the Lord will answer me. Who can stand if Thou wilt not pardon iniquities? Who can search out the matter of the Lord? Who can question His decree or His judgments? For vengeance belongs unto the Lord. I will wait patiently and rest for You will revive my soul.

Psalm of Deliverance 2

I am delighted to be remembered by my God. Can God forget the creation of His hands? Will He forget His children as captives in the hands of the enemy? I will rejoice for You have dealt bountifully with me. You remembered me in my misery and sent Your word to deliver me. My delight is in the word of the Lord. In Your word does my mind meditate day and night. I remember affliction and discipline and I am delighted that You spared not Your rod of love. It is Your rod that assures me that You are Father and I am Your child. I wait patiently on You, for though You wounded me you will yet heal me. Heal me and I shall be healed.

Psalm of Deliverance 3

I will sacrifice to You the sacrifices of praises and thanksgiving. I will delight myself in You. I meditate on the testimonies of Your goodness. You will not fail me. You will complete the good work that You started within me. I am delighted to be called by Your name. I will meditate on Your goodness and faithfulness. Though pestilences shall rise, though serpent's tongues arise, I will trust in You. You silence every accusation of the enemy. You set a new you song in my mouth. Many will see it and fear the LORD. It is the song of Your deliverances. You have delivered me from the lowest pit. Though I was in engulfed in trouble and sorrow, yet You were with me. My burdens rest assure on the shoulder of the Messiah. You bore my sorrow and diseases. You heal my mind and broken heart. I am but a dust before You, nevertheless Your preserve my soul. My days are numbered in Your book. Preserve my name in the book of the living. The blood that atoned for my guilt has preserved me. I am ever grateful for Jesus my Rock. You are a strong defense in time of trouble. I will meditate upon You all day long. Let love and passion for Your word whelp up within me once again. Let me put on immortality and let corruption be crucified with You this day. Sustain my soul and I shall live.

Psalm of Deliverance 4

I delight myself in You. Though I have seen many troubles, I am grateful for this journey that ever brings me close to You. Nothing shall separate me from Your love. This can only mean that every fiery trial that enters my life will purge me, sanctify me, and affirm me for Your kingdom. I am not of this world. Let these words comfort those for generations to come: God hears the prayer of the afflicted and is near to answer. I will quiet my soul to hear what the LORD will say. You word sustains my soul. I delight myself in your presence. Your presence is love and joy. I continually seek to embrace Your lot for my soul. You are for me, not against me, so I lay fear to rest. I am yours.

Psalm of Deliverance 5

Though sorrow endures for the night, joy comes in the morning. Many a times my tears rolled like a flood in the night watches. I was oppressed on every side. Iniquity pressed heavy upon me. I remember Thy mercies and trust in the work of the Christ. We have a Mediator before God. I delight myself in You.

In righteousness You punish. Though the hand of the oppressor is heavy upon me, You will deliver me. Their feet is set in slippery places, but I will remain steadfast on the Rock. I will trust You my fortress in time of trouble, in Your name. You sustain my soul in the midst of trouble. Though I was night to sleep the sleep of death, Your name sustained me there also and Your word delivered me. I delight myself in Your promises. You have done great things. My soul is overwhelmed with trouble, but You still sustain me. I will yet praise Him and my countenance will rejoice as you lighten my darkness. Trouble may endure for the night but joy comes in the morning.

Psalm of Deliverance 6

Come near me to deliver me, oh LORD. My enemies cast lots upon my soul. They seek to devour me. As a den of lions they lurk for my soul. They are as ravenous wolves, seeking to kill, steal, and destroy. You are the Good Shepherd. You give Your life for the sheep. Your little flock remains steadfast in the bosom of Jesus. You put a shield of protection roundabout as You encompass us with songs of deliverance. Day and night You set a watch upon my heart. I can rest assure that You will deliver with a mighty strong hand. Save me and I shall be saved. Deliver and I will be delivered. Your sheep know Your voice and obey not another. Day and night, night and day, they follow You and they will discern an impostor. Give me the ability to discern rightfully Your word. I was surrounded by ravenous wolves who took counsel against me. They set traps and snares for my soul. Destroy the snare of the enemy. Let them be disappointed and confounded. My days are numbered in Your hands. You have not left me at the mercy of the enemy. Because I am not utterly destroyed I am confident that You are with me. The snare will not hold me down, but You will deliver. As a bird is escaped from the snare of the fowler, so my soul will be delivered from death. A day declares unto the next the mercies of the LORD. Great is thy faithfulness! Let Your people rejoice and declare Your faithfulness from generation to generation. I am crucified with Christ nevertheless I live. You will quiet my soul by quiet waters and fill my soul with the fat of the land. I will continually feast on Your faithfulness. Your goodness declares Your love. I will hide myself in Thee until the storm passes by. Many are those that have troubled me, but You are by my side. The world receives us not because though we are in the world we are not of the world. These innumerable troubles give me the confidence I belong to You. Peace be upon us because of Your great work! My mind is stayed upon You. How I love to meditate upon Your faithfulness!

Psalm of Deliverance 7

Cover me in the shadow of Your wings. I remain steadfast upon Your word. Your promise sustains my life. Your word does not return void, but will accomplish that which is sent out to do. Let all those that love the LORD rejoice in Your steadfastness towards us. You will not abandon us but send us the Comforter. You are with us even unto the end of age. A day declares unto the next; Great is Your faithfulness. You are greatly to be praised. Your presence encompasses me as a fire. I am safe in Your steadfast hand. Though I shall stray from the Father, You disciplined me in love. You encourage me in my deepest pain, and You cover me with hope in my deepest despair. Though I have seen trouble, I behold Your grace. It is because of You that we are not consumed. Satan has asked You to swift me like chaff, but You prayed for my soul. Trouble may endure for the night, but joy comes in the morning.

Psalm of Deliverance 8

As a child that looks to the hand of her mother for care, so my soul looks to You for Your sustaining grace. I am nothing without You. I would be lost in the darkness of confusion without Your sustaining grace. Help my unbelief this day. Without faith it is impossible to please You. I resolute in my soul this day; God is not only a promise maker but a promise keeper as well. His word does not return void nor is it empty. Trust in the LORD and be of good courage. Fear must leave in the name of the Lord Jesus. Peace be upon you; You will see the faithfulness of the LORD and be filled with gladness. I will rejoice and be glad in You.

Psalm of Deliverance 9

Rebuke the devourer. I long to see a reward for my Labor. Not the reward of man but the reward of the LORD. Fires have tested the work of my hands, and all such that was not built upon the Rock was devoured in smoke. I contend with my heart this day; not my will, but Yours be done. I will no longer build what You have not called me to build. I would longer give my time to the devourer. Let idolatry fall in my life this day. I trust in the name of Jesus, my strength. How could I forget the love of my soul? I want to build with You. I want to love my enemies like You do. I want to bless those who curse me like You have taught me to do. I want to return good for evil. I want to no longer despise the day of small beginnings. I want to follow Your image of humility. I don't want to sit with the scornful or sit in the counsel of the wicked. They despise Your name and do not regard the fear of the LORD. This day I will seek Your wisdom. You overturn the wisdom of the wicked. Every weapon that was formed against me does not prevail. This is the heritage of the children of the LORD. I am counted among the righteous because of Your name. I will not sit on the table with those who have defile Your name. I will seek You with those who honor Your name. Your presence is my delight. Make no tarrying, but deliver me oh LORD.

Psalm of Deliverance 10

It is good that I consider the number of my days; for who can tell the matter? Many a times my foot was in the mouth of the grave, but You have spared my life. I am content to consider You all of my days. I am but a mist. Let me remember to count my days. I will not lift my soul to another. Let my hands do the work of a restorer. Let the ruins be built once again. Let my hand be as the hands of a warrior. Let the idols be destroyed once again. Let me be fierce for Your righteousness and truth. Let me equally despise the ways of the wicked. Let me be an instrument of Your love. I submit myself once again to You. I will obey You and Your name will I serve. I will not serve the lust of the flash, nor the pride of life, nor pursue the greed of desires. I will not seek to build my dream, but to choose whatever lot You have designed for my life. Many a times Your lot encompasses suffering, but whatever time I am afraid, I will trust in You. My sins have put a wall between me and You, but let the work of the Messiah demolish it today, and build me up once again for You are the Restorer. I resolute myself to this work that You do; Christ in me, the hope of glory.

Psalm of Deliverance 11

Come to me in my sorrow and sustain me. I am longing for You more than those who mourn in the night, that wait for the end of the night watches. Rescue my soul from the pit of hell and from despair. I remain steadfast in this one thing; great are Your mercies O LORD. I am troubled on every side; fiery darts encompass me all about. I am weary from my groaning and night watches. My soul has seen war. I am satisfied with Your presence. As a dry land longs for water, so my soul longs for You O LORD. I am still in Your remembrance; Great is Your faithfulness, O LORD. I will encourage my soul in the midst of trouble; I remain steadfast upon Your word. Though trouble threatens to cut me off from the land, of this one thing I know for sure; my days are in Your hand. I am not desolate nor left destitute, but I feast on the fatness of Your word. I am in bounty and not in lack. You restore me because of Your name's sake. I wait patiently on the Lord.

Psalm of Deliverance 12

Come to me in my distress. Hold on to me through the terrors by night. Lighten my darkness so that my soul is not given to confusion. A double minded man is unstable in all of his ways. Make me of one mind. Let my delight be only in You. Let my soul and my heart be on only for You. I despise the idols that have laid a hold of my life. Bring my soul back to You. I will love You with all my mind, all my heart, and all my strength. I will not lift up my soul to another. Let my worship come on out of an undivided heart. Not by might nor by power, but by Your Spirit.

Psalm of Deliverance 13

I will trust that You will lead my life. You are the Author of my destiny. You cover me with light and break off confusion from me in

Jesus name. Jesus is the Light of the world. No one hides a Light under a bushel, but it is brought forth to lighten the night. I have been covered in confusion many a times, but You have always been the way out. You light up my path. I resolute in my heart not to walk the broad way that leads to destruction, but the narrow path that leads to life. Let me not be confounded by my enemies, for it is Your name that they hate. I am delighted to bear the image of the Christ. Let my mind be that of the Christ and help me to bring every thought captive into obedience. I am not my own, but I am the workmanship of the Messiah. Let me bear the fruit of Your word; Righteousness, peace, joy, love, faith, goodness, gentleness, long suffering, and humility. You brighten my darkness. You set me free from the snare of confusion. Let everyone who trusts in the name of Jesus be set free today from the snare of confusion.

Psalm of Deliverance 14

I come to You as a living sacrifice. I have known adversity. You are familiar with my weakness. You are aware of the secret storms; You are familiar with my sorrow in the night watches. Redeem my soul. Innumerable enemies have risen against me. I pour out my complaint before You for vain is the help of men. The help of men disappoints, but in You I will never be disappointed. You are not like man that You should lie. Yes, let every men be counted a liar and God be true. I will not heed to the seducing doctrine of demons, but delight myself in the truth. Jesus said: I am the way, the life and the truth. Truth has come to set me free. Though men press on me on every side, Your promise preserves my life. Though many take counsel to ensnare my soul, I entrust the keeping of my soul to You. Commune with my heart to be still; I will be still and know that You are God.

Psalm of Deliverance 15

I am not troubled when evil men prosper in their way and they advance against me. I behold their end; for they are set in slippery places. You sustain the outcast and heal the wound. Heal me and I will be healed. Deliver me from my oppressors for they are stronger than me. They cast my soul down, but yet You sustain me. It is because of Your loving kindness that I'm not destroyed. A day declares unto the next: Great is Your faithfulness. I pray not for me only O LORD, but for my enemies as well. Let them receive the revelation of the Messiah. Let their darkness become light. Forgive them for they know now what they do. There is a way that seems right to a man but in the end leads to destruction and death. Jesus You are the hope of glory.

Psalm of Deliverance 16

It is good for me that I praise the LORD. His praise shall be ever on my lips. Though darkness has covered me, though fear has overtaken me, yet I will trust in the name of the LORD. I go about mourning my complaint before the Most High. I wait patiently to see what the LORD will answer. My hope is in God all the day long. Night and day, day and night are my thoughts directed towards You. Let the meditations of my heart be acceptable unto You my LORD. I will yet praise Him when I walk through deep valleys. Even darkness will become light around me for You are ever with me. The darkness cannot comprehend the light that comes forth from Thy presence. Wait patiently upon the LORD, and again I say wait patiently.

Psalm of Deliverance 17

Many are those that rise up against me, O LORD. Deliver me and I shall be delivered. I am in love with Your word. Your word is my delight and my hope all the day long. I waited for You and You heard my cry. My tears have been gathered into Your bottle. I am counted with the righteous because of the name of the Messiah. You are the word that became flesh and dwelt among us, but we did not regard the hour of visitation. We were all like sheep gone astray, everyone to his own thing and his own thoughts. I regard the number of my days so that I meditate upon You all the day long. I long for You that You may refresh me as a dry land is refreshed by the rain. I am resolute in my heart this day to be still before You. Clothe me in righteousness and write Your name upon my heart. Let my delight be in You and may I continually be ever before You. When I walk through fires You are with me. You will never leave me nor abandon me. In the day of trouble I will consider the work of Your hands and examine my ways before the LORD, for in righteousness You correct. All Your judgments are truth. It is better to fall into the hands of God than in the hands of man. Innumerable troubles have pressed sore upon me, but You deliver me out of them all. You are my hope and my salvation, and my song all the day long.

Psalm of Deliverance 18

Come to me and regard my low estate, for I have sinned before You. Shall He who created the eyes not see; shall He who created the ears not hear? Innumerable evils have engulfed me. I will not touch the unclean thing but present myself before You this day O LORD. Oh that Thou will heal me from this disease of sin. O that this flesh may be crucified with the Christ, no longer to live according to its will and desires. I come to You so that I may no longer walk according to the former things, for a new thing You do this day. Your mercies are new every morning. You behold me in the light of the Messiah and separate me unto You. Let holiness arise in me, let love continue, let peace abide, let purity be the fragrance of my offering. I submit myself to the sprinkling of the blood, for the propitiation of my sin. Christ in me, the hope of glory. Come to rescue me.

Psalm of Deliverance 19

I am delighted to call upon You with those that love You and seek You in sincerity. There is a remnant that shall consecrate themselves unto You. Those that will not take Your name in vain or sit on the seat of the scornful. They do not sit at the table with the wicked nor regard the counsel of the proud. They seek You in the morning, and in the evening their meditation is directed upon You. They regard You in all their decisions and all of their ways. They lie awake in the night watches pouring out their complaint before You. They regard not the ways of the proud. They dwell in secret places with You and feast upon Your word. They meditate upon Your goodness and faithfulness. They emanate Your light in a wicked and perverse generation. They mourn the ways of the wicked and are filled with grief at the ways of the wavering child. Justice is in and all their judgments for they discern willfully according to Your heart. They spare not the rod of correction from their friends. They bless their enemy and remain steadfast in the midst of contempt. They are not moved in the day of trouble for their feet are steadfast upon the Rock. I will call upon You together with such that call upon You out of a pure and undefiled hard. Blessed be the name of the LORD.

Psalm of Deliverance 20

Bless the LORD O my soul and all that is within me and forget not all His benefits. For He set my feet upon the Rock and when the storms come I shall not be moved. You are a defense and a strong tower for my soul. The humble will hear and consider. You are with me in trouble to deliver me. Though war rages without, peace dwells within. I will be still and know that You are God. Bless the Lord for all His marvelous works. Their mysteries are beyond the understanding of men. His might covers the earth; His name cuts through bars of iron. He has come to deliver captivity. Let eyes be opened, let the ears be opened and tuned into the good report of the LORD. Let the name of Jesus the Messiah deliver my soul. For I was near to be slipped in the pit of death. Hell sought to cover me and to claim my days. But I can now dwell in safety with You for Your name has been my defense. I have seen the strength of the LORD deliver me from the lowest hell so I will yet praise Him all of my days. Bless the LORD O my soul and His marvelous name.

Psalm of Deliverance 21

Commune with my heart this day to rest in Your completed work. Christ in me, the hope of glory. I surrender to Your great love. Thank you for the grace and the gift of faith. I will trust no other name to deliver my soul. I resolute in my heart that the keeping of my soul is in Your hand. You complete the good work which You have started in me. I am not troubled, for though I fall Your hand will uphold me. I will yet praise You for You have strengthened me. You breath upon me anew and empower me. Your Spirit raises up a standard against the enemy. Though sorrows may come, though heartache may pierce, yet I am continuously comforted by Your Spirit. I abide with You in this place, and surrender my heart to the Comforter. Your thoughts will always be so much higher than my thoughts, and Your plans so much better than my plans. I rest in You this day. I let myself be overtaken by You and for You. Lead the way and I will follow. Commune with my heart to be still.

Psalm of Deliverance 22

I have seen the wicked prosper in his way. As a fool was my soul grieved and considered not the ways of the LORD. It is better to trust in the name of the LORD than to put confidence in princes. The wicked regard not the ways of the LORD nor is the fear of the LORD in their regard. Their counsel is darkened and yet the go not about mourning their sin. They regard lying lips and the counsel of the ungodly. They think that the LORD will not hear, but the LORD sits on the throne and laughs. He confuses their plans so that they may not prosper in their wicked devices. The wicked is overtaken in his own net. This will take place so that the name of the LORD may be feared and reverenced. Though His anger may last for a moment, He is quick to hear the prayer of the humble and contrite. For whosoever will call upon the name of the Lord will be saved.

Psalm of Deliverance 23

How long O LORD will You turn Your face from avenging the oppression of the wicked and the unjust? How long before You set captivity free? How long before You cut the cords of the oppressor? How long must I go about mourning in our low estate? I considered my ways before the LORD in the days of my affliction. For surely in righteousness You have afflicted. You have given us into the hands of the oppressor for we have swayed from Your ways and polluted the habitation of the LORD. We did not regard Your pleas of correction. We did not humble ourselves in the day of the visitation. Why do we go about mourning in the day of trouble when the LORD disciplines? Shall we continue to prostitute the grace of the LORD? Should He not take vengeance on our idols? Should He not regard the wicked counsel in secret? Should He not inflict vengeance upon the corruption of our soul? Is He still not a loving Father that disciplines us?

For this one thing I know for sure; though You have wounded me, You will heal. You will devour the devourer, and when you will pardon me You will direct Your anger towards my oppressor. I am grateful that I can draw near to You have through the Messiah; For there is no condemnation to those who are in Christ Jesus, who walk not according to the flesh but according to the Spirit. So take vengeance LORD upon the works of my flesh and the interventions of my heart.

Psalm of Deliverance 24

I am grateful for the new beginning that I have seen in You; Christ in me, the hope of glory. As the clay in the hands of the Potter, so I resolute myself into the hands of my Creator. Create in me a clean heart O God, and a steadfast spirit. Help my feet be firmly established in the ways of the LORD. For I can do no good thing apart from You, but I behold the Messiah crucified. I am healed from this poison of sin. I am delivered from the wicked man that I am. I have regarded the pierced Messiah and trusted in His appropriation for my sins. I am not moved by those that regard not Your name nor honor You. I have been given a new name, a name that resembles with my new identity in Christ. I rest in the finished work of the cross, for even death has been swallowed up. I rest in You.

Psalm of Deliverance 25

Anew song You have put in my heart and upon my lips. Many will hear and fear the LORD. Your testimonies are sure. They sustain me through the rocky places. I will not stumble but trust confidently in the name of the LORD. I will be delivered from the snares of the fowler. I shall tread confidently upon scorpions. Because I have loved Your name, You will deliver me and not forget me in the hand of mine enemies. You still have me in remembrance and are with me in trouble. I cried to You and You rescued me. You heard my groans from the lowest pit. When evil men sought to cut me off and my days are set to rest, yet You deliver my soul. You numbered my days and my breath will ever be upheld by Your word. Your promise sustains me in the pit of death. Though they cast lots against me to wound me, the LORD sustains me. You will heal my deadly wound. You will revive and You will restore. Return back unto the LORD with your whole heart! The day of His visitation is at hand. The righteous will hear and rejoice. They will regard the way of the LORD. Though wicked man rise against me, the LORD will be round about me as a wall of protection. My soul is in the keeping of the Messiah. I drink the new wine of the new covenant; Your blood spilled for my guilt. The Messiah has become the guilt offering that stands between the Father and me. He has become the Light in which to Gentiles rejoice. You will not cast off forever, for though trouble may endure for the night, joy comes in the morning.

Psalm of Deliverance 26

Your judgments are righteous, O LORD. I dare not lift my face against the anger of the LORD. For as a fool I regarded not the counsel of the LORD but have sought out my own ways. My wisdom has become foolishness. I was greatly in derision. I perceive that God has handed me over to the wicked counsel of mine own heart. Then I cried out to the LORD. O LORD, will You be angry forever? For in foolishness I regarded not Your ways. I swayed from the fear of the LORD and I was covered with confusion. Oh LORD, please heal me. Leave me not as prey to my own ways and to my own thoughts. How can I be delivered from this corruption of my soul? What is the way of remedy for this wicked man that I am? I behold and see and trust in the name of the Messiah. You have come to set me free from this captivity. I will set no evil thing before mine eyes. I will not regard the lies of the wicked. I will not dwell upon the seat with the scornful or those that invent wicked devices. I will no longer go about in the counsel of mine own heart, but will wait for the answer of the LORD. I will regard You in all of my ways. Blessed be the name of the LORD.

Psalm of Deliverance 27

Come to me in my sorrow, You Lily of the Valley. You have known the ways of the mourner. You are grieved with wickedness every day. You are abhorred by our idolatries. You see the secret wicked counsels. You know our way from afar and need no one to tell You what is within man. For men is always inclined upon evil. Our ways are inclined to perdition. Our delights fall short of the glory of the LORD. Return onto the LORD all ye righteous. Seek Him while He may be found. Praise the name of the LORD and return to Him while He may be found.

Psalm of Deliverance 28

I am delighted when they tell me; Let us seek the LORD together. There is a people in a wicked generation who make their trust in the name of the LORD. They will not regard to ways of the wicked nor desire to sit at the table with devils. Their delight is in the LORD all of their days. They go about seeking those that regard the name of the LORD, and rejoice at the presence of the LORD. They sharpen one another like iron; they are in the hands of the Maker. They spare not the rod of correction but have their delight in the consecration of His great name. These are counted among the righteous. They delight not in a form of righteousness that is without power. They trust in the name of the Messiah. They call upon His name in the day of trouble. They trust confidently in Him and take refuge in His name as in a strong tower. They will never be ashamed. Ye who fear the Lord, praise Him. Ye who fear the LORD, seek His face, for it is good that we examine our ways. These are the chosen remnant in this generation. Let all who fear the LORD praise His name.

Psalm of Deliverance 29

Let not lukewarmness dwell within my heart, and let not indignation infect me. The LORD says: I counsel you to buy gold refined in the fire and return to your former first love. Your voice will I hear and regard Your counsel. Let a new passion whelp up within my soul. Let all that has put out the fire of zeal from my heart be cast to the side. For a flickering flame You will not put out, nor do You crush a bruised reed. You will revive me and uphold me with Your righteous right hand. I hope in You all the day long. Restoration is set upon Your heart towards Your people. May the righteous hear and rebuild again to desolate ruins. Let our hearts be illuminated by You as in the days of old. Let our hearts be set on simplicity and humble service to You. Let our high looks be brought low and let not our wicked thoughts prosper. But there is a people that will hear You and will seek You in the day of Your visitation. There is a people that are gathering oil for the day of their slumber. Awaken my love, O LORD. Awaken my passion for the Bridegroom, for near is the day of His return.

Psalm of Deliverance 30

Let my words be few and my ears regard what the LORD says. I will not be quick to bring the sacrifice of fools nor to partake of the strange fire. I will touch not the unclean thing so that You may receive me. I will come out from among them so that I may not receive of her plaques. Let my heart regard this day the counsel of the LORD.

Psalm of Deliverance 31

My tongue is as a pen of a ready writer. What can I say to You that hasn't been said before? My strength fails me. I am brought very low. I go about mourning all the day long. Your hand pressed sore upon me, yet will I praise You. You have wounded me with a deadly wound. I go about as a fool in counsel of my own heart and the imaginations of my own mind. Let me put on incorruption this day. Let my darkness become light. Let the raging seas be quiet. Help me relinquish all control. Help me to take refuge in Your great name. Let me never be put to shame. Those that make the LORD their trust will never be disappointed. Those who put their trust in Your promises will never be filled with shame. I go about groaning in my sorrow. Though the LORD wounded me, yet will He heal me. In compassion will He guide me with His council and afterwards received me to glory. As I partake in the sufferings of the Messiah, I am confident that afterwards I will be received to glory by the power of His resurrection. I am perfected in You. I behold the impurities of my soul in the mirror of Your word, yet I surrender to Your hand that ever fashions me in grace. I trust in Your unfailing love and Your matchless grace.

Psalm of Deliverance 32

Come to me all who are weary and heavy-laden and I will give you rest. I am comforted by Your invitation this day. I am relieved that I no longer have to carry this burden, though I will always have to carry my cross. I must deny myself continually and pick up my cross daily. I am not left to the mercies of mine enemies, neither is my cry hidden from the LORD in the day of my distress. I behold Your mysteries and wait for You here to hear what the LORD will answer me in the day of my calamity. Peace dwells within and abides deeply even in the midst of the raging noise and ravenous wolves. I am at peace though sorrow abides. You turn my mourning into joy. Tears whelp up in my eyes continually but You will wash away the pain of the past. Evil men rise to devour my soul. I will not fear. For what can men do unto me? Are not my days counted into Your hands? Are You still not a promise keeper? Are You still not the way maker? Are You not the one that opens and no man can shut? I resolute myself to be still today before the LORD; For I am yet visited by His compassion. I am yet fashioned into the image of the Messiah. I am yet remembered as a beloved one. You write my name upon Your palms so that You will not forget me. Though others may leave and others betray, You always remain Faithfull. I am continuously captivated by Your beauty. Your presence warms my soul. Your compassion comforts me in the day of distress. You take pity upon my soul for You remember that I am but dust. I press forward towards the mark so that I may finish the race as a faithful servant. I mingle not my heart with the affairs of this world so that I may be as a ready soldier. I cease all striving. Bless the

LORD O my soul for all His marvelous works.

Psalm of Deliverance 33

Oh LORD, how compassionate is Your lovingkindness towards Your people. Your love endures forever. You forget not Your covenant of old. There is a blood that has sealed my deliverance. It is not the blood of goats or of rams, but that of the sacrificial Lamb, the Messiah. What can deliver me from this wicked man that I am? What can sanctify me in Your mercies and grace? Praise be for the pierce Messiah that have suffered to bare my iniquities. Can a man cleanse his own way? For our hearts is inclined towards evil all day long. All our thoughts are but vanities. We regard not the Most High in our thoughts. We have all gone astray, we have all sought our own ways. But the LORD took pity on our frame. It pleased the LORD to prepare a way of salvation for us. Many will hear and see.

Let our hearts be turned from wickedness and our imaginations and idolatries. Restore innocence into our inner heart so that we may rejoice at the work of Your hands.

Psalm of Deliverance 34

Come to me in my hour of suffering. Draw near to my soul for formed weapons threaten to destroy me. My soul goes about mourning. Where is the LORD? The LORD is near to the brokenhearted. Innumerable evils have overtaken me. The enemies throw threats at me all day long. If the LORD have not been for me I would have long ago been counted among the dead. But it has pleased You to deliver my soul. I have been regarded as an outcast, yet the LORD has received me. I cry out to You because of the hand of my mine oppressors. They press heavily on me all day long. They throw nets upon my feet so that I may stumble; yet You uphold me. I will feast with You in the midst of mine enemies. They laugh at the day of my calamity, yet the LORD will uphold me. You sent trouble to surround them as a fog. You let their counsels be confused and You let their wisdom become foolishness. Because they regard not the LORD nor fear His name, You will remember them in the day of mine visitation. They take counsel in secret to overthrow my ways. They are high and lofty, yet they will be brought low. I trust in Your name. They will not see their desired end upon my life. Praise be to the LORD for yet He is the sustainer of my soul.

Psalm of Deliverance 35

You dwell among the weak and lowly. You remember the poor and uplift them. You uphold the orphan and the widow. You regard the outcasts of the land. You uplift them out of the pit of despair and sit them at the table of abundance. You surround them with comfort in the day of distress. You see

the hand of the oppressor and regard it. There
is a day of visitation when You will bring
vengeance upon the wicked. Take vengeance
upon them and deliver the poor. Regard the
prayer of the destitute. All those that trust in
the LORD, praise His name.

Psalm of Deliverance 36

There is a secret that I have found. I delight
to visit with You often in this place. Come to
rescue me aand deliver me from all evil. Do
not let wicked men prosper in their ways
against me. Let me taste of Your assurance in
this place, for I will yet praise Him when He
will bring me out into a large place. There is
no limit to what Your mighty hand can do. I
remember the testimonies of old and meditate
upon them day and night. Let all such that
seek my life be enlightened with the light of
the Messiah and the countenance of Your
love; for I will yet bless those that have cursed
me. I will yet forgive those that have wronged

me. I will not fear their threats. If I live I belong to You, whether I die I belong to You. Deliver me from their threats by Your hand so that they may perceive the hand of the LORD. Regard not their lying accusations or their slanders. They seek to devour every good thing from my soul. Arise O LORD and let the enemies be scattered. They are more than the number of hairs on my head. I take refuge in You for in justice You deliver my soul. You uphold my feet so that I do not slip nor sleep the sleep of death. You overturn their feet in their pursuit of my soul. I delight myself in You, my Redeemer and Savior. Praise ye the LORD.

Psalm of Deliverance 37

There is a stream thereof that rejoices the city of God. It is a living water that satisfies the thirst of my soul. I go yearning as a parched land. I will yet know abundance as the refreshing of the rain. Penetrate the crevices of this parched heart. Soften the clay of this hardened soul. Break up again the fallow ground. Work through in me the seed of Your word. Let hope again flourish in me. Let faith arise into the unseen. I rest into the hand of the Messiah, for You will complete the good work which You have started in me. As the rain comes into a desert place, so Your Spirit comes to refresh my soul. You turn to dry valley into an abundance of streams. I will praise the LORD for all His marvelous works.

Psalm of Deliverance 38

I contend with my heart so that I may not sin before the LORD. For the LORD hates the ways of wickedness but has compassion on the lowly. You show me the way and lead me in the darkened night. Even confusion clears out in Your presence. I crucify my need to understand and I trust. For surely You will not abandon the works of Your hands. Surely You will not deliver me into the hands of mine enemies. As a bird is escaped from the cage, so is my soul escaped from the hand of the oppressor. You dwell with me in lowly places and refute those that seek to set snares for my feet. Yet I go about mourning for their soul. In the day of their calamity I cried to You with tears. I returned good for evil, yet they have not regarded the day of Your visitation. They hid their faces from You because all their thoughts were evil before You. You searched out their ways as they gather prisoners of the soul. You despise their doings. Yet a new song is risen within me. It is the song of the redeemed. I turn to You and behold not the way of the wicked. You are my God and early will I seek You. I will not fear what men can do. I will not despair because of the hand of the oppressor; For yet I will sing the song of freedom. I will praise the LORD.

Psalm of Deliverance 39

I wait for the redemption of the corruption of my soul. Early will I seek You. Will the dead praise You? But my foot was night to the grave. My soul yearns for You. Deliver me from the strong bondage. Shatter my idols, my ways, and my dreams. Let me emerge as a brand new creation. Captivate me in a brand new way. Saturate me in Your presence. Revive me again from the sleep of death. Quiet the noise that seeks to steal peace. Let me find You on my knees again. Let my mouth praise You all the day long. Let all my thoughts be inclined in Your ways. Let all the sorrow be turned into joy. Let all the heartache be healed now in Jesus. Let my mind be healed in His name. Let depression subside in the joy of Your presence. Let confusion clear out in His great, matchless name. Let anxiety be put to rest in Your presence. I surrender to You, matchless LORD; for You are my King.

Psalm of Deliverance 40

As the night waits for the morning, so my soul waits for Your faithfulness. Your faithfulness heals me of the hope deferred. I will no longer trust in idols nor put my hope in things that disappoint, but I put my hope in You all the day long. I await for the day of my redemption. From whence comes my help? Is it not from the Maker of heaven and earth? Is it not from the Maker of the night and day? Have You not created the stars to shine in darkness? Have You not created the moon to shine the darkened path? So is my way lightened by Your word in the darkness. You will not suffer my foot to slip, nor my soul to sleep the sleep of death. I follow the Light through this deep darkness. You have never left me ever alone. I give thanks unto the LORD for His faithfulness endures forever.

Psalm of Deliverance 41

Why do You feel so far away? Why do stand so afar in the day of my mourning? Yet, I perceive that You are near to my heart. You heal the brokenhearted. You carry me in the day of my calamity and visit me in the day of my suffering. I sit to visit the testimonies of old. They are without number. Surely You shall deliver me from the noisome pestilence. A day declares unto the next; great are Your mercies oh LORD. You uphold the shattered pieces of my heart. You have set Your heart on delivering my soul. Who is this King of glory; the LORD, mighty in battle. O my soul, rest in the LORD, for I will yet trust Him. Though I have seen innumerable evils, yet will my praise be for Him all day long. Praise ye the LORD.

Psalm of Deliverance 42

You satisfy my soul. As a sheep feasts in quiet pastures, so is my soul satisfied with Your word. I feast on it continually and my soul is delighted in You. You prepare a place for me. I am overjoyed for You have received my soul. As a fool I wandered from Your presence, but as a Good Shepherd You sought out my soul. You quiet my soul in Your presence. You reassure me of Your love; such grace and such mercy. Who is this LORD that pursues my soul? I am overtaken by Your loving kindness. I hear Your promises anew. I await for the redemption of my body. Let my soul be glad with You in the new Jerusalem.

Psalm of Deliverance 43

Praises shall rise continuously before the LORD. You are the Maker of heaven and earth. You are the one that sets the sun to rise up. You are the one that has made all the creatures. You have fashioned me in my mother's womb. All my days are written in Your book. You feed the sparrows of the sky; You who dresses up the lilies of the valley. You who never miss a beating of my heart; You who always counts my tears and my hurts. It's You who never left me alone in this fight. It's You who has upheld me when others wish I die. When sorrow filled my heart through kisses of betrayal. It's You alone oh LORD that helped me up again. Though I have seen sorrows and pain has pierced my heart, my song remains directly Unto the LORD my God. Praise be unto the LORD.

Psalm of Deliverance 44

I am not alone though fear has overtaken me.
I will put my trust in You for it is good for me
that I trust in the LORD. I direct my
countenance towards Your face. I am helped
in the LORD; I am not forsaken. Why are you
afraid oh my soul? Trust confidently in the
LORD for His faithfulness will refresh You
again as the morning sun. Has He who
created the ear not hear? Has He who created
the eye not see? The LORD has known me in
the day of my affliction. He has visited me
with the song of deliverance. It has pleased
the LORD to uphold me in the day of my
trouble. Were it not for the LORD on my
side, I would have been left desolate. There is
a hope in the day of calamity. Great is Your
faithfulness, oh LORD. Your goodness
reaches unto the heavens. I consider the
works of Your hands for they are without
number. Your thoughts towards me are
continuously for good. I delight myself in the
works of Your hands. It is good for me to

perceive the work of the LORD and to delight myself in Your testimonies. Your promise sustains me in the low pit. You deliver me from the devastation. You preserve my soul when the sword lies on my throat. You deliver from the impossible situation. You comprehend my innermost being when I am wounded by the judgments of my closest friends. I am set in a place of bounty. My soul continuously feasts upon You; For who has sustained me in the day of my trouble? The LORD, the LORD Almighty. Let peace abide in my soul through the Messiah Jesus. Praise ye the LORD.

Psalm of Deliverance 45

Hope is the anchor of my soul. I am anchored into the promises of the LORD. Though I am slayed, yet will I trust in Your unfailing love. I lean not upon my own understanding. You work in ways that we cannot perceive. You create the pastures and the quiet waters. I rest here with You because of Your unfailing love. Don't delay oh LORD to deliver me. I have known the gift of long-suffering. I have endured through valleys and hills. You upheld me when my marrow was dried up. You anchored my soul against all unbelief. I believe in spite of the impossible. I surrender for You lead me in Your will. I consider my ways whether they please You; search my heart oh LORD. Lead me into Your promises Father. Wipe off the tears of unbelief. Dry out the waters of bitterness. Come near when I am weak. Breathe life when I am downcast. Hold me steadfast when I cannot cling. Stand still my soul and trust in the LORD, for His promise remains yes and amen.

Psalm of Deliverance 46

Awake oh my LORD, awake my soul from the slumber of death; for I am devoted to You. I raise my soul not to another. I delight myself in You and in Your word. In Your word do I meditate day and night. Let not my heart be entangled with indifference. Let me not fall in lukewarmness. Help me to return to my former first love. Let me not become desolate and destitute. Let me not avenge myself upon mine enemies; but I will rest in You while You make mine enemies Your footstool. I am worn out with trouble. My knees become weary with my groaning. I go about as one cast off from Your presence; then I perceived why Your hand pressed sore upon me. Let us repent and return unto the LORD; for He takes vengeance upon our inventions and idolatries of our hearts. You remember the covenant by the sprinkling of the Messiah. It is because of Your grace that we are not utterly consumed. Awaken my love from the slumber of death. Renew my passion with the zeal of truth. Lead me again into Your inner courts. Let me feast upon the goodness of the LORD, for You will yet save me in Your unfailing love. Praise ye the LORD.

Psalm of Deliverance 47

I am refreshed in Your unfailing love. I am delighted when they tell me: Come, let us seek the face of the LORD. Your face LORD will I seek. Remove my stony heart and give me a heart of flesh; for it is my sin that has taken me afar from Your presence. I remember the days of old and I go about mourning for my soul. As a fool did not I regard Your treasure, the hidden treasures of the night. Boldly I come before Your throne of grace. I remember the works of Messiah, the Christ. Jesus has torn the veil of partition. Boldly I come with a renewed sense of faith. Christ in me the hope of glory. You unclog my stony heart so that the rivers of life can flow again. I belong to You forever because of Your great name. My name is written in the Book of the Living. Give thanks unto the LORD for all His marvelous works. Early do I rise to seek Your face. In the evening still my prayer shall be inclined unto You. I give thanks to the Maker of heaven and earth for He has considered the low estate of His handmaid.

Psalm of Deliverance 48

I am delighted to dwell with the saints, with those that call upon the name of the LORD. Set sincerity upon our hearts; let not love de defiled. Give us an undivided heart. Let one regard another in a higher estate. Let Your name be magnified in our midst. May we stir one another to humility. May we serve one another in love. May our hands work together to build for Your name. Let all that we do be pure and sincere. Let all that we say be seasoned with grace and love. Let patience abide and not pride or strife. Let all be sincere without setting snares. It is good that the LORD has gathered us under the shadow of His wings. He keeps watch over His flock, redeeming us from the pit; For ravenous wolves seek to scatter the sheep, but the LORD will defend us by His great name. The sheep will obey Him and follow His voice. Jesus, the Good Shepherd will carry His little flock in His bosom. You will present us without blemish unto the end of age. His work is that none of the sheep may be scattered. Let all that have breath praise the LORD for all His marvelous works.

Psalm of Deliverance 49

Oh LORD, how long will it be before You answer my cry for help? For evil men take counsel against my soul. They set snares for my feet so to cause me to stumble. They lurk in hiding as a lion seeking to devour its prey. They sit with the scornful and they sharpen their tongues against the innocent. All their thoughts are continually set on wickedness. They devoured the needy and the poor. They lie in wait in order to take souls captive. They puff up in pride thinking no one will regard. They despise the cry of the needy thinking that there is no helper; But You oh LORD are my help all day long. I go about mourning my complained to You. Let them not prosper in their plots towards my soul. Let me be delivered from the hidden snares. I will yet praise Him for my soul will find comfort and a strong Deliverer in You. I lift my praises to You continually. Surely You shall deliver me from the hand of the strong oppressor. You lift the needy out of the lowest dungeon and set them up for a continuous feast. You take vengeance upon the schemes of the wicked men in order to deliver out of their hands. Oh LORD, take pity on mine enemies that they may consider the works of Your hand. Let their eyes be opened as the sunrises after the night. May they come to know the love of the Messiah, Jesus Christ. Deliver their souls out of the captivity of the enemy. Deliver their souls from the torment of pride. They have fallen into the pit they have dug up for others. Deliver the weak out of their hands. My Helper keeps watch day and night. I rest confidently knowing that when I awake I shall dwell in safety. My soul is set in safety up on a high place. The wicked do not understand and pursue in vain. Your name is a tower of strong defense. Let all who hear understand.

Psalm of Deliverance 50

Why I must I go about mourning all day? Why must I continually dwell in the house of mourning? Then I understood that it is good that I have been afflicted by Your hand; My soul receives correction and I will understand. It is better to dwell in the house of mourning than in the house of feasting; so I will regard the fear of the LORD. I will take notice of the steps of my goings. I will examine myself by Your word. Oh LORD, You know my inner thoughts. They are not hid from You. You fashion me continually and mold my heart. Such wonderful privilege to have Your hand at work in my soul. The suffering pushes me closer to You. I take notice and regard Your word. There is a joy on which I feast continuously in my soul. It is the joy of salvation, the joy of having a righteous soul. I thank You again for the work of the Messiah; Jesus, the righteous Prince in me. You once again make the crooked paths straight. You once again level out the low valleys. You were

a man of sorrow and pain. You were pierced
for my transgressions and pride. I am grateful
for the work You do in my life; for as a fool I
often wonder from Your ways. You put
sorrow in my path so that I may return back
unto You; for there is no peace for the wicked
that stray. Praise the LORD and the Messiah
of my salvation.

Psalm of Deliverance 51

I meditate upon Your testimonies of old;
How great is the works of Your hands. They
are beyond understanding. If I was to behold
them all the day long, they are beyond
searching out. Such thoughts of the Most
High are beyond understanding. For who can
know the mind of God or understand all of
His wonderful mysteries? I meditate upon
them day and night. My thoughts dwell upon
Your beauty. Such marvelous works are too
great for me; For I am but a man with a
measure of grace: increase my measure to

receive more of grace. I rejoice in You all of the day. Praise Him for all of His marvelous grace.

Psalm of Deliverance 52

Rest here my soul, rest confidently in the help of the LORD; For the LORD will not forsake the work of His hands. Though trouble pressed me on every side all day, my heart is at peace in this place. Your mighty hand watches continuously over my soul. My ways are not hid from the LORD. He perceives the intentions of my heart from afar. He surrounds me with correction and love. Were it not for the LORD, I would have long ago slipped; my foot would have long ago slipped in the pit of destruction. But You take pity upon my soul. You guide me by Your Spirit with counsel and truth. You deliver me out of the hand of the enemy. You silence the lying tongues that speak continuously. You cover me with the shield of faith; You are the armor that I put on this day. Some may trust in horses, and some may trust in chariots, but I will trust in the name of the LORD. Rest confidently oh my soul, for the keeper of your soul neither slumbers or sleeps.

Psalm of Deliverance 53

Remain hidden in this place of safety. Let not your heart be troubled anymore. For many are the trials of the righteous, but the LORD will deliver us from them all. A day declares unto the next Your faithfulness. You remain steadfast by Your word. Your word is alive and accomplishing its purpose. I am not troubled though mountains shall quake. You still the raging anxiety within my heart. Peace comes and my heart obeys. Let not my heart behold the ways of wickedness and desire its dainties. Their table is a snare; but I feast continuously on Your unfailing love. Let the Messiah, the Prince of peace rest upon my heart. Oh my soul, be at rest, for you shall dwell in safety.

Psalm of Deliverance 54

I consider the work of Your hands; the stars and the moon and the sun and the rain. I meditate upon the mysteries of Your creation. Who is this King of glory of immeasurable wisdom? I see the birds as You feed them by day; they never cease to sing songs of praise. For all creation praises Your name. My Maker sees me each brand-new day. You're there to provide, deliver, and heal. Your hand fashioned me just the same. You breathe upon me life and know me by name. Why are you anxious on my soul? Will the Maker forget the work of His hands? Trust confidently in His name, for the Maker of all creation will uphold You all of your days.

Psalm of Deliverance 55

My ways are not hid from the LORD. My heart often deceives me; for there is a way that appears right unto man but the end of it is death. Who shall deliver my soul from this death? Jesus the Messiah is the only way. Search my heart oh God and set my feet upon the road to salvation. Let my heart hold in fear and trembling this salvation. Lead me into Your perfect holiness. I will rest confidently, for my soul is now escaped from death. There is a broad way that seems right unto men, but the end of it is destruction. Blessed are those that found the narrow way of salvation.

Psalm of Deliverance 56

Weapons are forged against my soul, but this one thing I know; they shall not prevail. Your word wars against the inventions of wicked man. Why are you afraid oh my soul? Just be still and see His mighty hand. His word will accomplish it. A day will declare unto the next; the word of the LORD lives forever with power and reign.

Psalm of Deliverance 57

Some may put their trust in wisdom, some may trust in science, some may trust in systems, some may trust in men, but I will trust in the name of the LORD. When troubles come, I am not moved neither do You suffer my soul to be afraid. I dwell in the dwelling place of safety and grace. Because I have trusted in Your name, You sustain me. I love Your name all day long. You are my shield and tower of defense. Whom shall I fear in the day of distress? Though the mountains may quake and the oceans may roar, I am steadfast in the name of the LORD. My heart will bring a sacrifice of worship unto the LORD. I put my trust in His name. This shall please the LORD. I regard the faithfulness of the LORD and will not be afraid. O my soul, obey this day. Trust in the LORD all of your days.

Psalm of Deliverance 58

What is man that You are mindful of him? What is man that You should consider him? Yet it pleased the LORD to dwell with those of a low estate. You consider the state of the human heart and perceive that is wickedness. It had pleased the LORD to make a way. The Messiah is the way of salvation this day. All who trust Him will never be the same. You renewed my heart, my mind, and my soul. Such a mystery; who can understand? You continually set a watch upon my heart. May You find pleasure in my service this day. May I walk before You with an upright heart. May I seek to put on Jesus daily; Not in my own power, or wisdom, or flesh. It is by Your Spirit and the works of Your hands. Create in me the regenerated heart and put Your Spirit of love and truth upon my heart. Direct the footsteps of my life so that I may walk uprightly before the LORD; for You have accomplished is by Your will. You will show mercy upon whomever You will. Let me consider the work of Your hands and regard Your truth in reverence. It is good for me to give thanks unto Your name.

Psalm of Deliverance 59

You never cease to amaze me again and again; For when there's no way of escape, You escape me by Your hand. I consider Your ways. Give thanks oh my soul all of the days; For You have not failed me, and never You will. I cast imaginations and disappointments down. I want no longer seek after what leads astray. Idolatry is broken in Jesus name today. I am escaped from sorrow, from snares, and from despair. Deceiving voices now are silenced in Your name. Seducing spirits flee where Jesus is proclaimed. Doctrines of demons crushed, where truth alone abides. My soul is now escaped from the deceit of doubt. Confusing voices come to steal away my peace. I am resolute to find the truth that shines the way. Messiah please guide me today

and always; soon You will return to take me
to the prepared place.

Psalm of Deliverance 60

Let all those who labor unto the LORD, cease
your striving, your crying and tears; For the
LORD surely will reward. The fire will test all
that you build; That which remains standing
only is unto Him. Do not spend your time
building that which He has not said; For the
day will come to test it. Build upon the Rock,
the sure foundation. When Jesus is uplifted
rewards will follow after. Don't stir one
another to foolish ambitions and pride; but in
humility and love serve others. Oh my soul,
take notice in which manner you build before
the LORD. Be not quick to offer the
sacrifices of fools. Do not bring before Him
strange fire. I take counsel with the truth. Let
all I do be pleasing unto the LORD. Let not
your right hand regard that which the left
hand has done. Let not your service be before

the eyes of men. Let everything be done without vainglory or strife. Go into Your closet in secret seeking the LORD, and the LORD will reward you openly. Praise Him for His endless grace.

Psalm of Deliverance 61

Oh my LORD have mercy, LORD have mercy on me! My soul is greatly in derision. Confusion has covered me as darkness. I go about mourning mine iniquities before the LORD. I have behaved foolishly before the LORD. In ignorance did I stray from His ways. Your rod of correction was not spared from my ways. With love and compassion You lead me into Your righteousness. I am comforted by Your grace. For though I may fall, Your grace will sustain my footing. You lead me in the path of Your grace. You restore because of Your name's sake. Though iniquities have overtaken me, yet You preserve my soul. You remember that I am but clay into Your hands. My heart looks to You as the clay looks to the hands of the Potter. Fashion me into the image of grace. May the Messiah emerge in my thoughts continuously and so I find my rest into Your covenant of grace. Your words are like honey upon my lips. They are pleasant to me and in them do I make my delight. Though I was sore stricken with a deadly wound; yet You will revive me. Continue to become my delight all the day. Uphold my footing with Your righteous right hand. So I will perceive the faithfulness of the LORD. He will not allow me to know the way of perdition; For You alone sustain my soul. I cried out to You for my soul is vexed in derision. I have strayed from the LORD, yet in Your compassion You lightened my path. You make the crooked paths straight. I am comforted by the work of the Messiah. He is the Mediator between the LORD and men. Let faith arise in a brand new way, for new pestilences have stricken me down. I have also known the noisome pestilence and the terrors by night. I wait upon You all the day long. Will the LORD cast off forever? For You have made a new covenant with me. Early will I rise and consider the works of Your hands. Sorrow fills my heart, but I behold the Christ. Oh, who will save me from this wicked man that I am? Praise be unto the LORD for His saving grace. My delight is in the Messiah, the Lamb. He has become my delight all of the day. I am not forsaken but redeemed by grace. I behold the Christ to be healed from my deadly wound. You uphold me in the place of transformation. My soul is emerged into a brand-new creation. Such knowledge is too wonderful for me to understand. Give thanks unto the LORD for His mercies and grace.

Psalm of Deliverance 62

Oh LORD, cover me in the day of the battle. I am surrounded on every side. They take counsel against my life. They said: There is no helper for her soul. But I will put my trust in You. I will lean upon You in the day of distress; for my cry was not hid from Your sight. The LORD has taken notice of my cry; So be turned back men of iniquities. The LORD is my helper and shield. He will not leave me destitute, but surely He shall deliver me. He has put a new song upon my lips. It is a song of rejoicing in Him. Your name will be my shield and buckler, and now You have become my salvation. How can I go about mourning in doubt? The LORD is near to those that call upon His name. His hand is not short that He should not deliver. My heart, trust in the LORD for He is the shield of your faith: I resolute myself to be still in His hands. You set a watch upon my mouth and upon my ways. The Sustainer of my soul neither slumbers nor sleeps. He is attentive to the ways of my feet and is quick to fill me with strength. I have made my bed into a pool of water. Tears flood my eyes, yet the LORD comforts me. How could I behold such marvelous works? In iniquity I have been fashioned, yet you reshaped me into a vessel of honor. I hold this treasurer into a jar of clay. Redeem me oh LORD, and I will be redeemed. Let my soul praise Him, the joy of my countenance and the shield of my faith. Praise ye the LORD, for it is good to give thanks unto the LORD.

Psalm of Deliverance 63

I am in great distress, oh LORD. The enemy has caught my foot in a snare. I am lead astray into a darkened pit; But from the low pit did I raise my voice of mine supplications. Have mercy upon me. How long will You delay? Will the dead praise You? Will You forget the works of Your hands. Cover me as a shield of defense. For lying tongues have risen up against me to tare me to pieces; But yet I trust in Your unfailing love. Surely you will set me free from the snare. The Messiah has risen from the dead. So raise me up with You from the low pit of hell. You hold the keys of the abyss and death. Oh LORD, have mercy upon me. I need You all the day long. I stray from Your ways as a fool that is drunk. I'm covered in shame because of my pride. But Your grace will find me and as of bright light You lighten my path. You will not suffer the enemy to condemn. You cover me in the sprinkling of Your grace. Such knowledge is too wonderful for me to understand. Deliver, and I shall be delivered. Save, and I will be saved. Bless the LORD O my soul and all that is within me for He will yet redeem my soul from the lowest hell.

Psalm of Deliverance 64

I am attentive to what the word of the LORD will speak. I am firm in my decision to walk into His ways. I wait patiently and receive rebuke of the LORD; for in grace He corrects me with love as a compassionate Father. I am not afraid of the day of tomorrow for the LORD has set a guide upon my feet. The Messiah is the way to the Father. I am not alone for You will not abandon me. You uphold me continuously in Your righteousness. You suffer me not to stumble nor sleep. You are as a consuming fire. I long to dwell with You continuously. I awake early to hear what the LORD will speak. Though often Your hand pressed sore upon me, nevertheless You uphold me by Your righteous right hand. Let all those who hear understand; For Your righteous work is a great mystery. My way was not hid from Your face. You told me: Seek my face. Your face LORD will I seek. Early will I rise to yet praise Him, the joy of my countenance. Praise ye the LORD.

Psalm of Deliverance 65

The LORD is near to those that call upon His name. So turn back mine enemies, for the LORD is the sustainer of my life. My soul is counted among the living. Righteousness is my portion of grace. You sustain me when evil men rise up against me. They seek to devour my soul as prey. They regard not the fear of the LORD; But because of the LORD they are turned back. They will not prosper in their ways, but the LORD will cut off their remembrance. You defend me as a shield of defense. You are before me and roundabout. There is no impenetrable way, for the enemy will behold me from afar. I am set in in safety in the hiding place. Such knowledge is too wonderful for me to understand. I considered the working grace of the LORD. I am not afraid when evil men rise up against me. You set me up in a place of divine safety from their hands. They will not dwell among the righteous for they considered not Your ways. They boast themselves against You great name. When You arise as a tower of defense, they are all scattered. Everyone is turned back from their evil intents. Praise ye the LORD, O my soul for He has considered your low estate. He has considered that You have been an outcast so it please the LORD to rise to your defense. Let the redeemed of the LORD say so. The place of my safety is in the bosom of the Messiah. I will give thanks unto the LORD. All the days will I sacrifice praises unto Him.

Psalm of Deliverance 66

Often I wonder, oh LORD have You shut Your ear unto my cry? For I go about mourning as evil men advance against me. They cast lots for my soul. They sharpen their arrows and surround me. Be a shield of defense roundabout me. Let me not fall as prey into their hands. Let me not fall the sleep of death. They have made plans to cast me down for they said there is no helper. Oh LORD, help me. Give me not over into their hands. Great are Your mercies; they are renewed every morning. I am greatly troubled. Though I am afraid, I will trust in You. They have afflicted as the hands of an oppressor. I was cast down and brought very low. O LORD, will You forget Your promises forever? I was as a fool. I stepped out of the LORD's will. Deliver me! Do not consume me now in Your hot displeasure. Your promises will sustain my soul. Great is Your faithfulness. Though the LORD has cast me off for a season, His steadfast love remains just the same. Though You have wounded me in Your anger, You avenge the oppressor of my soul. Come to deliver my soul from the lowest hell.

Psalm of Deliverance 67

I call upon You day and night. I am weary from my groaning. I wait for the redemption of my flesh. Early in the morning will I seek Your face. I can do nothing apart from Your unfailing grace. You sustain me by Your righteous hand. Innumerable troubles have come my way. The fiery trials purify me today. The blood of the Messiah is my shield of defense. I will raise my praise unto Your holy name. Come to me in my distress and be the joy of my countenance. My face is turned and fixed upon the LORD. Blessed be His name.

Psalm of Deliverance 68

I hunger and thirst after Your righteous ways. Surely You satisfy the longing of the heart. As the rain falls upon the parched land, so Your Spirit renews me every day. You are my delight all the day long. I am consumed with Your love. I taste of Your promise and I joy in Your love. I delight to know the depths of the LORD. Unveil mysteries into my soul. Let the depths of my soul hold You as a treasure. Come to me in a brand-new way. Reveal to me the hidden mysteries. Destroy the idols that are still in the way. Lead me into brand-new consecration. Crucified with Christ, nevertheless I live. I want to be set aside unto Jesus the Messiah. To taste of Your goodness, Your presence, Your promise. Let me behold Your faithfulness every day. Oh my soul, behold and see the good land. This is the portion of the redeemed of the LORD.

Psalm of Deliverance 69

My soul continuously feast upon Your word. I am fat with Your promise. You set abundance in my path. I am delighted in Your unfailing love. I lack nothing for I am ever before You. I am continuously in Your thoughts. Your plan for me is for a hope and a future. I resolute myself to lay aside my pride. Lead the way and lead my life. I lack no good thing for You provide all things. I am in a continuous feast of Your wander. When I awake You have been the keeper of my soul. I am delighted when they say; Let's praise the LORD.

Psalm of Deliverance 70

Hold me in perfect peace for the thought of my heart is set upon You. Let peace abide where righteousness dwells. I am ever held in Your unfailing love. I seek You but I often don't understand. Increase my measure to behold new insights of Your grace. Continue to dwell with me, so shall I be in safety. My soul longs for You in a weary land. Though many evils surround me, my heart is steadfast. You keep in perfect peace those whose mind is set on things above. My treasure is hidden with You for I am not of this world. I seek You in the morning, at noon time, and at night. My thoughts are continuously set on things above. Returning unto the prepared place. I dwell in safety even in the midst of death. I am continuously at rest because of Your unfailing grace. Praise ye the LORD as you consider the work of His hands.

Psalm of Deliverance 71

Sorrow comprehends my heart. I go about mourning day and night. My eyes are a continuous stream of water. When will You rise to be my help? I am left desolate in my sorrows. I am devoured as prey. My name is covered in darkness. Evil men take notice of my weakened state. They formed a coalition against my soul. They intend to cut me off from the land. But in You do I put my trust. Will Your word fail me so that I am not upheld? Though I am devoured, though I am castoff, though I am in a book with the forgotten, yet will I praise Him. His words will renew me all the days. Though I was cast off, yet Your word will sustain me and Your unfailing love revive me. You bring me into Your remembrance because of Your promises. This is my hope all the day long. Though the LORD cast me off for a season, He will yet perform His unfailing word. Great is Your faithfulness.

Psalm of Deliverance 72

Encourage yourself in the LORD and in His unfailing word; For the LORD is steadfast. Faithfulness is His name. He is not man that He should lie. Let every man be a liar, and

God be true. The day of the LORD is at hand. My eyes have seen the glory of the LORD. Holy is He! I redirect my thoughts to Your word. Though heaven and earth shall pass away, Your word remains the same.

Psalm of Deliverance 73

Joy is the portion of my life. I have tasted the lot of suffering, but joy comes in the morning. As I wait my soul is encouraged. Great is Your faithfulness oh LORD. Though for a moment darkness has covered me, You remain the same. I reverence Your name above all names. Joy is the portion of the righteous in the LORD. I meditate upon Your unfailing love, so will I sing praises. My heart rejoices for I am set aside, undefiled. Come to me as the morning sun that brightens the darkness. Let joy come and push away doubt. I will rejoice in the LORD for in Him there is no shadow of turning. Great is Your faithfulness oh LORD.

Psalm of Deliverance 74

As incense is continuously raised unto You, so is my prayer continuous before You day and night. I have known the watches of the night. There is One that beholds me and keeps me at night. Even in sleep my lips declare Your glory. Your testimonies are more than the hairs on my head. You satisfy my soul in the land of the weary. You give my soul sweet rest and joy. I am not forsaken nor will You will ever abandon me. I am now hidden in Christ. I dwell with You in safety. I am overtaken by Your sweet love. Rest o my soul and be at peace for the LORD has dealt well with you. His goodness has overtaken me in all of my ways. As a dove is hidden in the cleft of the Rock, so my soul dwells in safety. Each day is counted with the LORD. He upholds me by His righteous right hand. It is good for me that I might consider the works of His hands. Let my lips praise Him and my soul be hidden in Him; for I will yet behold His marvelous face in the land of the living. I am set free by his mighty hand. Deliver me from the noisome pestilence. Cover me with Your truth and so shall I be awakened to glory.

Psalm of Deliverance 75

Consume the dross of my soul away o LORD. I delight not in my own ways but in the way of the LORD. I am a sinful man inclined to evil, but the LORD has provided a way of escape. My soul beholds this truth and great mystery; The Messiah is risen from the dead. I am compelled by Your loving kindness. Your goodness leads me to repentance. I am often foolish and of no understanding. I am stubborn in my own ways, in pride; but this day I behold Jesus. Deliver me from this wicked flesh and doubt.

Psalm of Deliverance 76

Save me o LORD, for evil men have risen to devour my flesh. The Spirit is willing but my flesh is so weak. I am weary from the oppression of men. They seek to make my soul to stumble. Their hands are full with tools of destruction. They said: Who will deliver your soul from my hands? But I have regarded the Maker of heaven and earth. I cry to You all the day. Strength fails me as so does my flesh. My marrow has dried up because of my groaning. Evil men have surrounded me roundabout. Calamities have been multiplied. The hand of the persecutor is near. I tremble not at the threats of men. I trust in You when I am afraid. I lean upon the Christ in joy or in pain. I am afflicted and in need of Your help. Save me oh LORD, from the hand of the oppressor and heal my soul. Praise be unto Your glorious name.

Psalm of Deliverance 77

There is a work that rejoices the people of God. The hand of the LORD is near to restore. Let the ruins be rebuild again. Let the walls of protection encompass me about. As a shield of defense You veil me roundabout. Though innumerable evils are raised up against me, my soul is still at rest. It is finished in the Messiah. Here I am secure into Your hands. Restore that which the enemy has stolen. Recover all that I might have lost. Revive my soul by Your mercy and grace. Trouble is always with me, but I trust in Your name. Your unfailing love upholds me. Let all that trust in the LORD regard the restoration of the LORD, for He will recover that which has been lost. Praise His mighty name.

Psalm of Deliverance 78

Oh LORD, my soul is cast into the gull of bitterness. Sheol seeks to cover my soul. I cry out to You from the lowest dungeon. Will You forget Your faithfulness to me? I go all groaning because of my sorrow. The snare of the enemy has overtaken my soul. My foot slipped near to destruction, yet the LORD is still the sustainer of my soul. Even there shall Your hand uphold me. Even there Your Spirit is my guide. The darkness became as light roundabout me. Oh LORD, to You alone I cry. I looked for someone to take pity but I have found none. They form a coalition against me and defiled me day and night; Yet I will stand to declare Your faithfulness, and my mouth will be filled with Your praises. I found myself into the pit of hell, yet Jesus the Messiah will raise me up again. Let all who hear trust in the LORD.

Psalm of Deliverance 79

Let all that is within me and all that has breath praise the LORD; For He destroyed the destroyer and rebuke the devourer. All such that devoured have been devoured themselves. For though the LORD has cast me off for a season, yet He will revive me again. He perceived that in foolishness I strayed from His ways. When I was in the low dungeon I cried out to Him. Even there did the LORD regard my supplications. He repented of the evil that has done unto me and received with grace. Though evil seeks to cover me in death, there is a Mediator that stands before Your face. O LORD, have mercy on me. Let my soul rejoice in Thy salvation. Visit me again, so shall I perceive Your favor. Humbly do I direct my supplications unto You. Will the dead praise You? A wicked an unbelieving heart You despise; but I direct my trust into Your great name. So shall I be delivered from mine enemies and my soul will be delivered from the grave.

Psalm of Deliverance 80

All who find the way of righteousness bless the LORD; For He has warmed us by His countenance. He no longer numbers the evils of our ways. You cast them into a sea of forgetfulness. There is the Mediator between God and man: Jesus, the Messiah is His name. I found the way that gladdens my heart. Purity is in it. Salvation is its paths. It is not the blood of rams or of sacrifices that shall wipe my sins away: The blood of the Messiah, the Lamb has covered the penalty of mine transgressions. I will declare with my lips and with the testimonies of my life. I will teach sinners the way of salvation. I will direct the meditation of my heart to praise the LORD. Early will I rise to direct my supplications unto You. Though death has encompassed my very soul, I will put my trust in the name above all.

Psalm of Deliverance 81

Commune with the anxieties of my heart to be still. Confusion covered me as a frog, but Your truth abides above it all. I am not alone in my distress, for I perceive Your presence. Was it not for Your unfailing love that upholds me, I would have been long gone. Mine enemies long ago would have prospered against me, for they observe me all of the day. They sit on the seat of the scornful and pass unrighteous judgments against my soul. Violence is their very paths and their tongues are sharpened as darts of death. They lie with their tongues continuously. Mercies are not in their ways. They sit with the proud taking counsel against the innocent. They sit lurking in secret places someone whom they may devour. They come together to form a bond of death against my soul. They said: there will be no helper for her soul. They pressed sore against me on every side. Then I said: LORD, deliver my soul so that I not die. They treaded down on secret treasures. They observed my soul, my ways, and my troubles. They sought to build a wall between me and You; but now I perceive that nothing will separate me from Your love. They covered me with shame, despair, and sorrow but still Your hand will uphold me higher: Higher above the enemies schemes, higher above their plots and their snares. No one perceived the troubles of my soul, for new weapons were formed to destroy me. Still You uphold me with Your great love. O LORD deliver me from this place of death.

Psalm of Deliverance 82

Though I am surrounded by many evils, in You do I put my trust. Let mine enemies be turned back. Let their footing be in slippery places. They regard not with eyes of compassion. They are fully set on destroying my soul. They though no one beholds them and there is no helper. They spit words of threats and formed weapons of death. Into their hands I was for a season, but I remember the testimonies of old. It is good that I was afflicted, for my face has turned towards the LORD. Every single word of spoken condemnation I place at Your feet into Your washing stream. I am no longer devoted to my ways, but I am devoted to You, my King. All my days and all of my sorrows I place in Your hands. You behold all my tears. You take pity upon my sorrow, and deliver me from all that has pressed sore upon me.

Psalm of Deliverance 83

I love You with a perfect love because of Your correction. Though You pressed sore upon me, Your loving kindness do I embrace. My nights were filled with streams of water. No one perceived the trouble of my soul. Then I despaired and cried from my darkness: Deliver me oh LORD. Be quick to answer me for my foot is night to the grave. The gull of bitterness has engulfed me. There is an imposter in my heart. Deliver me from unforgiveness, bitterness, anger and strife. Deliver me from vain affections, pride, lust, jealousy, and rage. Deliver me from all the darkness and let the fruit of Your Spirit reign. I am not alone for You remain the same. You show me the way out by Your great compassion. You delivered me from the deepest pain. No one understands the weapon which evil men have formed against my soul. I cry out to You because of Your compassion. I am still at rest for I trust in the LORD.

Psalm of Deliverance 84

I perceived it pleased the LORD to visit me with His compassion. Early will I rise to give thanks unto His name. The weapons of the persecutor pressed sore upon me. Then I directed my cry out to You. You visit me with Your affection. Your peace flows as a stream of joy. Rejoice when others will persecute you, when others shall rise with lies just the same. Great will be your reward in heaven, for so they have treated the servants of the LORD that were before you; And when other shamefully entreat you, consider is not, for my grace is enough. My hand is still near and continuously with you. I fashion you in this place of hurt. Though darts of hate now compass you, I am a shield of love and of faith. I told you that one day you will be hated. It is because of my name's sake, not because of you. They hate you so much for they have even hated, the Father God that is above all else. They reject the truth because of their consciousness. Their hearts are filled with evil and hate. They transformed the glory into darkness; they surround themselves with others like them. They come together against the anointed; they hate the Son for their darkness is exposed. They tremble not with fear and reverence, but they hide in darkness and kill with their swords. The mercies of God are new every morning, but they will regard the persecutors' hands. I pray today LORD reveal Yourself to them, for they dwell like captives and are led astray. Tormentors now are being tormented. The hand of theirs masters is always near by. Their soul is captive to the darkness, yet they perceive not and trusted in lies. There is a way out for those that are covered in death and lies and deceit of hell. Jesus the Messiah is the way out; whoever calls on Him will be saved now.

Psalm of Deliverance 85

Continuous voices seek to drown out my faith, but the Author of my salvation upholds me each day. The LORD will not turn his back on me, but You always fashion me and cover me again. I am protected in Your love, for lies seek to drown my soul. Quietly I wait for the salvation of the LORD. Your truth puts to rest the voices of doubt.

Psalm of Deliverance 86

Deliver me LORD and I will be healed. My days are consumed with grief. Sorrow is always near. When my enemies dealt wickedly with me, my prayer was for them in their distress. I have not hid the way of grace from them, yet they did not regard and have done more wickedly than before. They despised Your forgiveness for they are proud. They think they need no helper, that they are gods. Your hand pressed sore on them, on every side, yet they still did not cry out. They remember not the days of old and how by Your hand the Egyptians were killed. Their strongest armies were drawn into death. Yet they say: Myths and fables, who is God that I should obey? Your compassion was for them for a season, but Your long-suffering will end for them soon. There is a time that the LORD will deliver; then He takes vengeance on wickedness. All that desire to taste of His freedom, must come now before it's too late. I am held safely in this place of freedom. I trust You now and in Your great name. Your spirit upholds me and cut the cords off. You cut through the bars of iron and hell. You show me the better way on which I must tread: denying myself and bearing the cross. I'm following Jesus for all of my days. Forever You uphold me by Your grace. Your grace is sufficient in my sorrow. When persecutions rise, I do not despair. You wash me in Your love and hide me from their faces. They asked me why I chose to trust in You the same. They have not received the way of salvation. They think by human strength and wisdom I stand. They did not perceive the hand that upholds me, nor did they seek to regard the LORD. They sit in confusion wandering intensely, at this great mystery that is before them all. What is this power; what is this wisdom? How can we cut you off from His love? But I cannot be separated from Your presence. My name is written in the Book of Life. Only the Lamb can break the seal, and write one to heaven and another to hell. For His will is that no one should perish, but soon He will take vengeance on pride. Children of disobedience, it's what they have chosen. They trust not in His name and continue in doubt. If only evil men would hear today, and consider their pride, and invite You inside. I thank You LORD that the oppressor cannot separate me from Your love. I trust You forever and always; I hide in You my beloved and crown.

Psalm of Deliverance 87

Nothing can separate me from Your love, though evil men persecute my soul. I am continuously before You. My ways are not hid from You o LORD. Will a mother forget her very own babies? Yet if this was to happen, You cannot forget. The persecutor is a tool of the devil. They are themselves captives at his will. They have given themselves over to darkness. They carry out the plans of destruction and death. They take souls captive with hot pleasure. They torment with their thoughts the innocent and poor. They form trials of rigged injustice. They pay evil man to bear false witnesses. When the accusations rise up in fullness, You will refute their lying tongues. I resolute myself to not fear them, but to trust in You and Your unfailing love. Though I am threatened with swords and chisels, I stand firm upon the solid Rock. Not in my own strength but in Your power. Your spirit gives me wisdom from above. I resolute myself to not think about it, the words I should speak when I am brought before. They all behold me with great wander: What is this power, what is this love? They throw accusations and mock me relentless, if maybe I'll give up and just obey. But I trust in You LORD, my strength and upholder; For when I am weak then I am strong. I lack no good thing in his place of darkness. I will bear witness of the Light. For I know for sure Your truth will abide still. Give me the wisdom to understand, to bless them in Lord Jesus, and not curse them, and to pray for those who despitefully use. To give them up into Your love LORD, for Your perfect love casts out all fear. Your perfect love casts out the darkness, casts out the hate, and fear with Your love. When madness sets in with its sorrow, You comfort me and carry me still. Your truth remains forever faithful; You cannot lie, You are not man. Release me now from the oppressor, the grip of death and den of hell. Remove the scales that blind their vision, in that they do not perceive the truth. Release them in the love of Jesus, Messiah King above all Kings.

Psalm of Deliverance 88

I abide in You with all of my heart and passion, for I cannot bear fruit on my own. You are my source of life and strength. Though evil men rise up to separate us, I am safely held in Your bosom and care. You considered my weakened estate; You have sent reinforcements by Your mercy and grace. Though every man has left my side, my Jesus remains the same, His my help. Fear of death has lead them astray. They have made covenants of death. If only their life could they escape now. They trusted in lies and their rewards are but pain. Have mercy on them that betrayed me this way. They have chastised me because of the Lord Jesus. Have mercy on my nearest friends that betrayed. They were disappointed; perhaps they will cry out. Perhaps they'll consider the ways and their paths. Perhaps just like Peter who betrayed you on that day, they too will find favor and repent from their ways. But I know king Jesus You are very near, a friend that upholds me and never betrays. I do not fear the invention of men, for You are with me within. I am covered in Your precious blood now. I rest here with You in the dens of death. You shut the mouth of the lions and snares. You devour the plans of wicked men. Come near to me all who are weary. I will call upon You in the time of distress. Forgiveness is set to break the darkness of unforgiveness and hatred of them. The bitterness of death compassed me, betrayed by even my closest friends; yet You sustain me in Your presence. I turn my face towards You and I'm saved.

Psalm of Deliverance 89

I have known sorrows immeasurable. I waited alone as the watchmen on the wall. Have you forgotten Your words and Your promise? As a fool I directed my words towards Him. The LORD is not slack of understanding. His hand is not slow so that He cannot save. His waiting upon you to trust in Him only, and to please Him with faith. This is the sacrifice I must offer; the steadfast faith in Your word and Your truth. You are so faithful LORD though fears and darkness, consume me now in doubt and pain. Release me now from this place of darkness. Cut though the doubt, the fear, and the shame. Release me now into Your promise. It is the work of the Christ in me that still stands. I hear the voices of doubt and failure. Rejection makes me a prisoner of pride. I hold on here for there is a Savior that will deliver me just the same. He has delivered before from the fowler. He hears my cries; His word will prevail. He sent His word to cut the cages, whose iron bars are doubt and pain.

Deliver me so I may sing LORD, Your faithfulness to every men. Let all the generations after consider now Your love and fame.

Psalm of Deliverance 90

Your glory fills the earth oh LORD. I am now delivered from the strong oppressor. For they persecute me daily in my heart. They set snares for my feet. Corruption is the work of their hands. Yet my prayer was for them in their time of distress. Your glory fills the earth o LORD, and darkness has become as a light about. I consider Your mighty exploits; For they are without measure. They cannot be counted. You also have been familiar with my sorrow. The ways of men the are not hid. Salvation belongeth to our Savior, Redeemer of soul and healer of life. Forever I'll praise You though now for a moment, I lie in wait for Your hand to save. I rest here now in Your presence; Your grace is sufficient, You love me the same. You have prepared a place of gladness. You call for my soul to take up the land of joy and wholeness. I hide forever in Your great name. Cover me now in this sojourning, my soul to keep forever near. For soon my Love and my Darling, will come for me my soul to raise. I am made new, such a creation, fashioned by love in the image of Christ. I got to the place prepared by my Savior, of eternal rest when I resurrect. I am welcome here because of my Savior; my crown of joy I lay at his feet. Forever I'll taste of Your sweet salvation, so I will worship You forever and always. You're the reason for my affections. I set my mind on things from above. When I shall be with You forever, others will read and understand. Rest oh my soul and love Him forever; my passions renewed I lay upon Him. I am delivered from the great darkness, and now I go to be forever with Him.

Psalm of Deliverance 91

I rise up early to give thanks unto the LORD. He who split the Sea and casts mountains down. He who feeds all things from His hand in love. He who covers all mine iniquities. He who opens doors and no one can shut. He who lifts me up on the eagle's wings. He who hides me in the cleft of the Rock. He was spared my life when death was near to me. He who troubles seas and makes oceans roar. He who my delight is become all day. He who speaks no lie but Truth is His name. He who knows all things and my inward thoughts. He who stills the seas and the winds that crush. He who calms all fears and anxieties. He who knows my ways and my wonderings. He who loves me still when I fall short. He who covers me in His precious blood. He who turns all things into steps of grace. He is who directs my steps and my plans. He who does not sleep but my soul does He keep. He who holds me still, and in doubt I hope. He who never leaves me all by myself. He is who restores what was lost, my Friend. He who holds me near in my broken state. He is who arises, when my foes have snares. He is who I need every single day. He is who I love more than anything. He is who I cry out to, when I am weak. He is who I trust when I am afraid. He who comes through when it seems like the end. He is who I need every single day. Every breath I breath as an offering, to Jesus my King with my thanksgiving.

Psalm of Deliverance 92

The LORD is compassionate to all who draw near. He understands the broken state of man. Jesus the Messiah comes to redeem, and make my soul whole again; I raise my song to Him. I give Him praises, thanksgiving is what I bring. For this shall please Him more than anything. Nothing else have I to bring unto Him, but my shattered heart with its hopes and dreams. I am so restless if my mouth withholds praises to my Savior down here below. Let all that's created sing praises to Him, for Jesus is Lord, forever He reins. I am of such little, little understanding, but still Your grace it upholds me. You comfort my sorrow and heal my despair, for in You I trust; there's no other way. You are the only way to the Father. He loves it when we trust the name above all others. I am not confused in this faith and grace; for I have known mercy underneath Your breath. I count all my blessings, renewed for me each day; For Your goodness and grace they will follow me. I give You my praise, a song shall I raise. I give You my thanks for each and every day. I rest here in Your hands, for safe I am here. You fight and defend me and You set me free. I raise declaration of Your deliverance. My thanksgivings are raised up from bellow. I know in sorrow, for near You were then. I've known You as my Friend and my only strength. I am delighted of the Father of love, for He calls me His and I am His child. I raise You new praises each and everyday, but words fail me now to declare it to Him. I cry tears of joy and tears of pain, but you always are and remain the same. My offering to You that I raise each day, is thanksgiving for this shall please Him always.

Psalm of Deliverance 93

I found the Savior in my despair. Jesus is the way, the Christ that came. I cry all my wailing, before Him I fall. He will deliver my soul and my heart. Often I tangle myself with cares, but Jesus my Savior loves me the same. He breaks me now free from snares that I've known, so now I sing praises to Him alone. He leads me to the Father, with gentleness He leads, protects me from the wolves, from snares, and from thieves. I know that His answer is always the same: I won't give up on you for I fight and defend. I am in Jesus hidden in Christ. I see that nothing can separate us now, for in Him my heart renewed each day. I know He defends me always the same. I am here below but I dwell with Him in realms above, above everything. I am not

alone in my trials and my fears, but He is the
risen Messiah that reins. I am resolute to give
You my heart for another I will not worship
now. I trust You the same and more each new
day, for You are the Light that heals my pain.
I am never alone: How could I deny Your
love that is holding me all of the time? I lay
everything down, the cares that press in. I
know You in freedom that comes from
within. Though caged I shall be for the love
of Christ, I still remain free inside my heart.
My conscience is sprinkled with freedoms of
grace; He understands me each and every day.
I lay all aside and follow Him home for soon
He will call me from here below. In that place
of tears, rejoicing shall be. I behold His face,
my Savior and King. Relentless I seek You;
each morning I cry. I trust that You carry me
all of the time. I am consecrated to His
matchless name. Jesus is my Savior, His love I
embrace.

Psalm of Deliverance 94

Your mercies are new with each brand-new day. Your covenant sure in Your matchless name. My passion shall be to know You alone, and to know Your nearness at the Father's throne. I call upon You; Hold me in pain, for enemies rise to devour the land. But I am unshaken for I am spoken for; Your armies You sent to defend my soul. Now I am devoted to You and Your cause, for You have remember Your promises now. I dwell in sweet places of bounty and grace. Your presence rejoices me every day. I am not alone, never will You leave. I praise my sweet Jesus and ask my soul to keep. My soul is in safety from things down below that have often tested my very core. I am not abandoned when enemies rise; You are great Father and I am Your child. Jesus lead me now into His embrace, and to the throne that is filled with grace; For He Himself will love me for this: that I trust in Jesus, the Christ that defends. I am forgiven; to You I sing all of my praises as an offering. Come in my sorrow and gladden my heart, for in heartache and pain I have known comfort that holds me above the sorrows that roll and battles each day that are here bellow. My prayers are raised as incense to You and as uphold them Your answer comes through. Your word is the delight of my soul, for with it You heal my broken heart. I rest all my crying Your joy to embrace. I pick up my cross and deny myself. My pleasures You are though sorrows I've known, as the persecutors content for my soul. I know that You always are Faithful, the same, for within You there is no shadow of death. I come now before You, my soul to entrust, into the hands of my Savior and God.

Psalm of Deliverance 95

My Lord and my Savior to You I submit; I offer You praises for in mercies You heal. You lead me with Your hand; Your counsel I know for now my ears open to You alone. My eyes they were darkened with veils of despair; You saturate me and breath life again. The lowest of hell I knew: this is true. Yes, there You revived me and raise me with You. I live forever with You by my side. I praise my Savior for now I have found, that You are Faithful and forever You'll be; I'll raise all my praises to You and Your name. I offer thanksgiving as a sacrifice, though words they will fail me to speak of Your heart. Such wonders, such mercy that follows me still; I rest here with You for I belong to You. You cover my shame that seeks to abide. You lift me with Your sweet tender embrace. I do not have words to give You my praise, for You deserve it with all of my DNA. Let every fiber that's woven within give thanks to Jesus, the Prince of peace. Let me speak praises to Him all my days. Let me give thanks to the LORD that still reins.

Psalm of Deliverance 96

Tranquility rests upon my heart, for the Prince of Peace comes to calm the storm. The voices that threaten to hunt my life are silenced by Jesus my Savior and crown. Leviathan rises to claim me to death; he is offended that he won't prevail. He claims the lives of those who in pride make covenants with devils that seek to bind. I am escaped from the death's despair, and now I am a risen with You up again. For who can save me from his mouth? Yet You have saved my soul from doubt. When death laid grip with its despair, I made my cry from lowest hell. How could I praise You for what You have done? No one would believe me though I testify; from despair's grip You raise me again. Jesus my Savior I'm Yours every day, for You have fashioned me as clay, a jar for Your honor so I rest my despair. Your treasures now I behold all my days, for You will fill me up once again. I am surrounded by angels that watch, and wonder such manner of grace I have got. I sing my praises to You all my days, for You have crushed the Leviathan's head. Death is arrested along with its grip. Fear is engulfed and lost in Your love. Let all who read really understand, for this is my testimony of His sweet grace. He did the impossible just for me, so I wonder if You cry to Him does He hear? He's no respecter of persons, oh no, and He saves the same all that Him trust. I'm not disappointed of this pain I've known, for in this wicked place, He still is enthroned. He open hades' pit with the key He holds, and does what He wants for He is God. Others will scorn me for these words that I speak, but I have seen the hades very grip. This is no fables I speak and I write, for he came to claim my very life. Jesus took pity upon my soul, for I have in foolishness spoken what I didn't know. He claimed me for heaven though I have seen, hell's very fire that raised from within. This is my story and this is my song, that Christ Lord Jesus raised me from abode. He claimed me for heaven; my name did he write into the book of living and life. He only Him does hold the power to break the seal for He paid with His life. I am resurrected though I should not be; If I was to tell you what I have seen you would believe that madness set in, yet live I by grace for I should be dead into the pit of hell. I wonder forever why my name He saved. I'll worship forever at His footstool of grace. Though words do fail me, my mind does comprehend, that I have known mercy in the belly of death; That I escaped hell's very pit, when darkness has covered me without escape. Yet You escaped me from the snare of hell. You crushed the Leviathan and shut up his mouth. My soul has known the place of hades. Many will hear and not comprehend. I was the one without escape, but still the LORD has provided a way. I should be counted with unredeemable, but You have still saved me though some laugh me to scorn. I am here forever seeking Your love. My praises to Him is all that I've got. I have nothing to bring but my wrongs again, when foolishness veiled me and cast me to death. I hide here forever in Your sweet embrace, for this is my song and what You have done. All that do hear me please understand, for what I speak is the truth, yet again many will turn into death's embrace, for they will fail to understand. Jesus is Lord and He reigns from on high, and I will forever lay down my crown. For He did save me from hell's embrace, though Leviathan still lurks in hiding to slay. I am forgiven and days You did add, so I give them back to You as a sacrifice. Hide me forever in the cleft of the Rock as a sweet lover that covers my soul. I am now going to lay aside the pride that so easily stumbles my life. I have known the sweetest of loves; Jesus my Savior He's on the throne. So I declare it, Him and Him alone. Let your soul now run from the hades of hell for there forever you will wail in pain. So call upon Jesus today and obey. Let all my praises never subside, but let them continue every day and night. I am forgiven and set free from here, the snares that were formed by monsters for me. I have understanding in Your sweet embrace, my Jesus, my Savior for You resurrect. It pleased You to count me with all of Your saints. Here I abide with You all of my days.

Psalm of Deliverance 97

I am escaped from the fowler's grip because of You LORD. You have in mercy destroyed the embrace from the ones that enslaves my heart. I give You praise, I give thanks for I am saved from death's embrace. You have in mercy heard my cry and I was helped by You for I am Your bride. I rest myself into Your embrace and I give You thanks; I always give thanks; For it is good for me to do this, for You now lead me to my destiny. I am released from the bars of iron that have bound me when they ensnared me. Though I still hear threats of despair, I'll trust You Jesus always the same. You are not slack that You should not save me, but You have allowed them to afflict me. So have I turned from my idolatries even though I known many calamities. I am not covered in darkness any longer, for there is a Savior, though hell has promised to seek my life and cover my name. Now I submit to the name above all names. I have now seen how foolish I have been, yet in Your wisdom my soul do You keep. When I awake my soul You do save for You did not slumber but watch me always. I am not given to death anymore; Keep a watch over me and my soul; Let my words from this day only speak, words that bring life and death's embrace. The LORD will heal me and raise me again though I have been wounded with sorrow and pain. I am resolute that from here on forth to give the LORD praise for all that He's done. For this is what pleases You more than all things, when I only trust in You and Your sweet embrace. Give thanks to the LORD all nations and birds, all creatures above and creatures below. Give thanks with your heart, with strength and your soul, for Jesus is Prince and He's on the throne. Give thanks to the Father that's up above, that pleased Him to bruise Him for my sins and your. Give thanks all ye nations for He is the King that rules above kingdoms and reins from within.

Give thanks all ye islands, and mountains, and hills, for His Your creator and ever He will be. Give thanks all ye birds that travel the skies, and praise Him with your song every day and all night. Pray Him all souls that have known His embrace, that set You free from hells very snares. Praise Him all ye saints that are washed in His blood, your very garments because of the Christ. One day the redeemed will forever sing the song of the saved from calamity; and with fear and trembling we'll cast down our crown, at the feet of Jesus, Messiah the Christ. The Father is pleased Him to honor His name, for He came to save us and raise us with Him. He came down in flesh for you and for me, for without Him death will have its sting. Praise Him that's created from smallest to great; let all that has breath declare of His grace. Heaven rejoices when one lost soul still embrace the Father and Jesus the Lord. Come with your praises every day, for each new morning new mercies remain. I am forever a sacrifice of praise to my Jesus for I am His bride.

Psalm of Deliverance 98

Entailed I have been with the cares of the world, but You lift the burdens, the cares and the hurt. My soul is set free for You to praise. Oh I love Jesus and the Father the same. You sent us a Comfort, Your Spirit to lead, to shows us the way into Your will. A place You've prepared for Your bride and soon You'll return for a brand-new life. A place You prepared of no suffering, where tears they will cease and pain is erased. I wait upon You prepared every day, and gather Your word in jars of clay. I rest here with You my soul to keep; I ask You to cleanse, renew and to save. The Spirit and Bride united they cry: Oh, Lord Jesus Christ, Maranatha.

Psalm of Deliverance 99

Let the masterpiece emerge in me my LORD, Your promised word. Let the pieces of my life cry You restore and You revive.

Psalm of Deliverance 100

I give thanks unto the LORD, for this shall praise Him more than many sacrifices. I am content when they tell me; Let's go to call upon His name, the Maker of heaven and earth. For though His anger lasts for a moment, He heals with pity all that trust in His name. Though You have wounded me with a deadly wound, I will yet praise Him. Though darkness will cover me, yet my song will still be directed unto His name. Yet though He slay me, I will yet praise Him for in righteousness He slays. His judgments are truth and righteousness. No one can challenge the decree of the LORD. His degrees proceed like lightings from His mighty throne. Yet it pleased You to take pity upon me and to deliver me. Give thanks unto the LORD for this is good.

ABOUT THE AUTHOR

Dorina Horvath is a servant of the Lord and is the founder of the non-profit foundation Outcry Ministries. She authored several books among one being "The Good Fight of Faith" and had written and released several music albums among being "Be Still" and "Deprogrammed". Her passion is to see the world changed and delivered through God's love one person at a time. No matter what your desperate situation may be today, whosoever will call upon the name of the Lord will be saved.

https://www.outcryministries.net
outcryministries333@gmail.com
YouTube –Outcry Ministries